A CourseGuide for

The Triune God

Fred Sanders

**ZONDERVAN
ACADEMIC**

ZONDERVAN ACADEMIC

A CourseGuide for The Triune God
Copyright © 2020 by Zondervan

Requests for information should be addressed to:
Zondervan, *3900 Sparks Dr. SE, Grand Rapids, Michigan 49546*

ISBN 978-0-310-11074-3 (softcover)

All Scripture quotations, unless otherwise indicated, are taken from The Holy Bible, New International Version®, NIV®. Copyright © 1973, 1978, 1984, 2011 by Biblica, Inc.® Used by permission of Zondervan. All rights reserved worldwide. www.Zondervan.com. The "NIV" and "New International Version" are trademarks registered in the United States Patent and Trademark Office by Biblica, Inc.®

Any internet addresses (websites, blogs, etc.) and telephone numbers in this book are offered as a resource. They are not intended in any way to be or imply an endorsement by Zondervan, nor does Zondervan vouch for the content of these sites and numbers for the life of this book.

No part of this publication may be reproduced, stored in a retrieval system, or transmitted in any form or by any means — electronic, mechanical, photocopy, recording, or any other — except for brief quotations in printed reviews, without the prior permission of the publisher.

Printed in the United States of America

CONTENTS

Introduction

Welcome to the *A CourseGuide for The Triune God*. These guides were created for formal and informal students alike who want to engage deeper in biblical, theological, or ministry studies. We hope this guide will provide an opportunity for you to grow not only in your understanding, but also in your faith.

How to Use This Guide

This guide is meant to be used in conjunction with the book *The Triune God* and its corresponding videos, *The Triune God, A Video Study*. After you have read each chapter in the book and watched the accompanying video lesson, the materials in this guide will help you review and assess what you have learned. Application-oriented questions are included as well.

Each CourseGuide has been individually designed to best equip you in your studies, but in general, you can expect the following components. Most CourseGuides begin every chapter with a "You Should Know" section, which highlights key terminology, people, and facts to remember. This section serves as a helpful summary for directing your studies. Reflection questions, typically two to three per chapter, prompt you to summarize key points you've learned. Discussion questions invite you to an even deeper level of engagement. Finally, most chapters will end with a short quiz to test your retention. You can find the answer key to each quiz at the bottom of the page following it.

For Further Study

CourseGuides accompany books and videos from some of the world's top biblical and theological scholars. They may be used independently, or in small groups or classrooms, offering quality instruction to equip students for academic and ministry pursuits. If you would like to engage in further study with Zondervan's CourseGuides, the full lineup may be viewed online. After completing your studies with *A CourseGuide for The Triune God*, we recommend moving on to *A CourseGuide for Faith Alone* and *A CourseGuide for Creation Care*.

CHAPTER 1

Attunement: *Gloria Patri*

You Should Know

- God revealed eternal, internal processions about himself in the missions of the Son and the Spirit.

- To reveal himself as Trinity, God joins explanatory words to his salvific acts.

- Theology can give an account of God as Trinity based solely on the incarnation and Pentecost

- Two biblical verses used in the *Gloria Patri* are Matthew 28:19 and Hebrews 13:8.

- *Gloria Patri*: the traditional name given to the prayer that begins, "Glory to the Father"

- Gerhoch of Reichersberg: medieval theologian who used the *Gloria Patri* to exposit Psalm 23

Essay Questions

Short

1. Prof. Sanders's goal, in part, is to bring theological clarity to the language of praise. Why is it important for the praise and worship used in the church to be theologically sound?

2. What does Prof. Sanders mean with the statement, "Theology is faith seeking understanding because it is praise seeking underpinning"? In what three ways does theology provide praise with what it seeks? State the answer in your own words. What are the three key moments in the development of the *Gloria Patri*, and how do they illustrate its connection to Trinitarian theology?

Long

1. A theme of this unit is that theology has a *movement*. It begins with praise to God for his gifts in salvation history, moves to understanding who this God is eternally, and ends with praise of the God so discovered. How does Prof. Sanders develop this theme in his discussion?

Quiz

1. What is Prof. Sanders's central contention in this course?
   a) The way God reveals the Trinity should determine how we form the doctrine of the Trinity.
   b) The Nicene and Chalcedonian Creeds are fundamentally biblical.
   c) Modern personalist philosophy offers great promise for understanding the interrelations among the persons of the Trinity.
   d) Evangelical theology needs to recover essential insights from the patristic era concerning the doctrine of the Trinity.

2. (T/F) The doctrine of the Trinity should not only be a conclusion of exegesis but should also inform the way that exegesis is done.

3. Why does Prof. Sanders refer to Trinitarian theology as a doxological movement?

   a) Because it begins with God's work in salvation history and moves to the principles behind this work, all the while giving glory to the three persons
   b) Because it surveys the learned opinion (Greek, *doxa*) of the Church Fathers
   c) Because it focuses its attention on the movement of love within the Trinity from Father to Son and back again, a love which comes alive as the Spirit
   d) Because it moves all over Scripture, assembling a God-glorifying doctrine from different parts of the canon

4. While not downplaying Scripture or verbal inspiration, Prof. Sanders makes what event of revelation central?

    a) Tradition of the church
    b) Experience of dependence on the divine
    c) The missions of the Son and Spirit
    d) The end-time Parousia of Christ

5. If Prof. Sanders calls the New Testament revelation the "irreplaceably primary theological witness," why does he also say that it is "indirect in its statements about the Trinity"?

    a) The Trinity is nowhere clearly revealed in Scripture.
    b) The actual revelation of the Trinity had already taken place in the advent of the Son and Spirit.
    c) The doctrine of the Trinity can only be inferred from the text of Scripture.
    d) The actual revelation of the Trinity had already occurred in the Old Testament.

6. What, according to John Webster, is the proper calling of theology?

    a) The praise of God by crafting concepts that turn the mind to divine splendor
    b) The explanation of God to believers that teaches true orthodoxy
    c) The contemplation of divine mysteries, such as the Trinity and incarnation
    d) The examination of the coherence of Christian belief

7. What is the main insight provided by the Christian doctrine of the triune God?

    a) What God manifested to us in Christ is the ultimate divine reality.
    b) The ultimate divine reality cannot be fathomed by human minds, because it is a mystery.
    c) What the Bible reveals about the internal relations among the persons of the Trinity can be discerned by attending to what the Scriptures imply about God.
    d) The doctrine of the Trinity preserves Christian uniqueness.

8. Among the different types of liturgy, what makes doxology unique?

    a) Doxologies are always structured in a Trinitarian way.
    b) Doxologies are hallowed by ancient use in the church in a way other types of liturgy are not.
    c) Doxologies are directed to God, while benedictions are directed to the worshipper.
    d) Doxologies make the leap to theology proper.

9. What spiritual instinct was typical of prayer in the early church?

    a) The proper role of humility
    b) The need for church-taught language in regulating theology in prayer
    c) The simultaneous reach toward glorifying God and toward explicit Trinitarian language
    d) The threefold ascription to God of the adjective *holy*

10. What does the *Gloria Patri* speak to God?

    a) The psalms
    b) Blessings requested for other Christians
    c) The language of revelation first heard from God
    d) The invocation of the Spirit

ANSWER KEY

1. A, 2. T, 3. A, 4. C, 5. B, 6. A, 7. A, 8. D, 9. C, 10. C

CHAPTER 2

Revelation of the Triune God

You Should Know

- Revelation is necessary for knowing God exists as a Trinity.

- Leonard Hodgson argued that the doctrine of the Trinity arises from human reflection on God's acts rather than directly from revelation.

- According to Karl Rahner, when the transcendental crosses over and becomes categorical in human experience, divine self-communication happens.

- The economy of salvation (or, the events of salvation history) is Karl Rahner's starting point for the doctrine of the Trinity.

- A theology that is hospitable to Trinitarian doctrine must maintain, in contrast to many modern theologies of revelation, the inner unity between act and word.

- J. Gresham Machen is an early twentieth-century Protestant who argued for the inner unity of God's actions and his verbal communication.

- J. I. Packer is a midcentury evangelical theologian who insisted that God's revelation is essentially but not exclusively verbal.

- According to J. I. Packer, divine speech is necessary for the inherent meaning of the salvation events to cross over into our sphere.

- The two-testament canon: the witness to the God of Israel who sends his Son and Spirit

- Divine interactionism: the notion of divine action in the world that Karl Rahner rejected

Essay Questions

Short

1. Why does Prof. Sanders argue that a doctrine of the Trinity should be the foundation for the doctrine of revelation rather than the other way around, the doctrine of revelation being the foundation of the doctrine of the Trinity?

2. What difference does a biblical theology of mystery make for understanding the revelation of the Trinity?

3. Compare the theology of revelation advanced by J. Gresham Machen with that of J. I. Packer. What do they have in common? In what ways do they differ?

Long

1. Compare and contrast how Leonard Hodgson and Karl Rahner relate their understanding of revelation to the Trinity. What is their common weakness, and what response does Prof. Sanders make to it?

Quiz

1. What makes knowledge of the Trinity possible?
    a) A mind disciplined by Christian virtue
    b) The Father sending the Son and Spirit
    c) Theology that is based on biblical exegesis
    d) Authentic love for God

2. What makes the doctrine of the Trinity more than just one item on a list of things that God has revealed?
    a) The doctrine requires a theology of redemption.
    b) The doctrine requires a more disciplined theology than other aspects of Christian teaching.
    c) The doctrine presupposes a community of faith to proclaim it in mission.
    d) The doctrine is not merely a doctrine but God's self-revelation, becoming present in a direct, intense, and personal way.

3. What was Karl Barth's starting point in his doctrine of the Trinity?

   a) The experience of suffering in history and its connection with the cross
   b) The data of the Old and New Testaments
   c) The fact that God reveals himself as Lord
   d) The eternal procession of the Son and the Spirit

4. What is the purpose of the two-testament Canon?

   a) To show forth the Trinity in clearly expressed formulations
   b) To provide the necessary history of ancient Israel required to understand the mission of Jesus
   c) To bear witness that the God of Israel spoke conclusively in the Son and the Spirit
   d) To show what sort of moral virtues should characterize the people of faith

5. One advantage of aligning the mystery of the Trinity with the biblical-theological understanding of *mystery* is that such an approach will protect what?

   a) The importance of Christian experience as an ancillary aspect of Trinitarianism
   b) The unity of Scripture
   c) The distinctions among the persons of the Godhead
   d) The separate missions of the Son and the Spirit

6. According to Leonard Hodgson, how is the doctrine of the Trinity derived?

   a) It is a divine revelation, disclosing both God's works and words that explicate those works.
   b) It is the product of rational but human reflection on specific revealed acts of God.
   c) It emerges naturally from Christian experience of redemption and worship.
   d) It is the result of Greek categories of philosophy influencing Christian theology.

7. What dilemma results from attempting to base the doctrine of the Trinity on the experience of God?

   a) The attributes of God would be limited to God's communicable attributes, while the essence of divine being would be completely unknowable.
   b) The focus on experiential revelation would lead to epistemological relativism, while the absolutizing of experiential revelation would lead to the supremacy of human subjectivity.
   c) The unity of God's actions would lead to an undifferentiated oneness in the Godhead, while the diversity of God's actions would lead to a proliferation of divine persons without limit.
   d) The eternal procession of the Son from the Father could not be established, while the different modes of acting as Trinity would be undifferentiated.

8. On what does Karl Rahner base his understanding of revelation?

   a) The *a priori* fact of God's existence
   b) The unity of the three persons as Speaker, Spoken, and Speaking
   c) The doctrine of the logos pervading the cosmos
   d) The structural openness of humans toward the divine as a condition of all experience

9. What are two key elements of *Dei Verbum*'s doctrine of revelation?

   a) God making known his will and establishing the Catholic magisterium
   b) God establishing the Catholic magisterium and speaking to humans as friends
   c) God making known his will and providing a preferential option for the poor
   d) God making known his will and speaking to humans as friends

10. J. I. Packer argues that what is necessary for understanding the meaning of a divine action?

a) Illumination of the minds of the witnesses
b) God's own communication
c) The magisterium of the Catholic Church
d) A creedal explanation

ANSWER KEY

1. B, 2. D, 3. C, 4. C, 5. B, 6. B, 7. C, 8. D, 9. D, 10. B

CHAPTER 3

Communicative Missions

You Should Know

- The Son and the Holy Spirit is the culminating point of the divine self-revelation.

- Because Trinitarian revelation involves the divine persons communicating themselves to each other, it is not only verbal, it is also conversational.

- Friedrich Schleiermacher is most known for establishing Christian doctrine on experience.

- Though experience cannot function magisterially over a doctrine of the Trinity, it can function ministerially.

- The ministerial function of experience is a motivation for trinitarian biblical interpretation.

- In Scripture, God testifies to the historical sending of the Son and the Spirit.

- As revelation, the Bible should be located in the doctrine of the Trinity.

- Rule of Faith: a summary of the key ideas in Scripture with an indication of their interconnections

- Irenaeus: early Christian theologian who used the rule of faith against Gnostic theologians

- B. B. Warfield: early twentieth-century theologian known for his defense of Scripture and the Trinity

Essay Questions

Short

1. In what sense are the missions of the Son and the Spirit communicative acts? How are they both self-interpreting and mutually-interpreting?

2. The Son and the Spirit speak the meaning of their missions to us, but they do this because they first speak that meaning to each other. Explain the mystery of the correspondence between the eternal conversation of the Trinity above us and the historical conversation of the Trinity to us.

3. What did B. B. Warfield mean when he claimed that while the doctrine of the Trinity was biblical, its revelation was in a peculiar sense not biblical?

Long

1. What is the proper relation between revelation and tradition? Are truths of revelation ever communicated through tradition and not elsewhere, so that tradition becomes an essential source of revelation? Are summaries of Scripture derived from tradition (e.g., the Apostles' Creed, the rule of faith, the Nicene Creed, etc.) necessary clarifications of biblical revelation, without which the meaning of that revelation could not be known?

Quiz

1. The actual revelation of the Trinity occurs in what?
   a) The propositional revelation of the Bible
   b) The missions of the Son and the Spirit
   c) The testimony of experience
   d) The insights of tradition

2. According to Scott Swain, communication is more than exchanging words; it is also what?

    a) A medium of historical insight

    b) A source of psychological exploration

    c) An activity that promotes social cohesion

    d) A matter of self-giving

3. As the culminating point of God's self-revelation, what do the Son and Spirit together show about that revelation?

    a) Its transcendent nature, exceeding all forms of human language

    b) Its inherent propensity toward inscripturation

    c) Its pervasive act-plus-word character

    d) Its personal rather than its propositional nature

4. On what does Friedrich Schleiermacher attempt to construct his theology? (p. 76)

    a) The presuppositions and implications of the consciousness of redemption

    b) The events of God in the history of salvation, along with their interpretation by human actors

    c) The unfolding theology of the Christian tradition

    d) The experience of unexplained and unredeemable suffering in the world

5. How did Karl Rahner attempt to give a more solid experiential basis to the doctrine of the Trinity than Friedrich Schleiermacher had? (p. 77)

    a) He correlated the subjective (experiential) and the objective (transcendental).

    b) He sought the human experience that is universal and not merely local or particular.

    c) He postulated a moral intuition that is trans-cultural and Trinitarian.

    d) He found a threefold movement in the biblical witness that he aligned with the Trinity's historical acts.

6. What is the main theological point made by Irenaeus when he presents a rule of faith that is Trinitarian in outline? (p. 82)

   a) The Gnostics have accurate biblical content but distort its correct order and connection.
   b) The doctrine of the Trinity is properly based on the rule of faith rather than another source.
   c) The true meaning of the words of Scripture is the Trinitarian meaning.
   d) The goal of biblical interpretation is to establish the authenticity of creedal statements already produced by tradition.

7. What happens when creedal formulas become independent of the biblical foundation and exegetical reasoning that informed them? (p. 83)

   a) They attain a form appropriate for inclusion in ecclesial liturgy.
   b) They become an obstacle rather than an aid to understanding.
   c) They become susceptible to heretical abuse.
   d) They inevitably support a Catholic hierarchy.

8. Why is a robust Trinitarianism best served by a transgenerational confessional apparatus? (p. 87)

   a) Because the kind of sophisticated articulation it requires cannot easily be elaborated by each generation on its own
   b) Because the church can do theology better when it acknowledges the role of past generations as mediators and guarantors of revelation
   c) Because the Trinity as mystery goes beyond the content of Scripture
   d) Because this is the best way to observe the biblical principle that parents should teach their children.

9. How can the statement, "We believe in the Trinity because Scripture teaches it" be analyzed and expanded into a fuller, more accurate statement?

   a) Scripture reveals the Trinity because of various passages that evince a Trinitarian structure (e.g., Matthew 3:16–17; 2 Corinthians 13:14).

b) The mutual interpretation of Scripture and the rule of faith make the doctrine of the Trinity clear.
c) The alignment of prophetic texts, messianic prophecies, and testimonies to God's Spirit implies the outlines of a doctrine of the Trinity.
d) Scripture is the authoritative account of the missions of the Son and the Spirit, who themselves bring the revelation of the Trinity.

10. How is the Scriptural revelation both ministerial and magisterial? (p. 90)

a) It is magisterial with respect to the missions of the Son and Spirit, but ministerial with respect to the church.
b) It is magisterial with respect to the missions of the Son and ministerial with respect to the mission of the Spirit.
c) It is ministerial with respect to the missions of the Son and the Spirit, but magisterial with respect to the church.
d) It is ministerial with respect to the ecclesiastical hierarchy, but magisterial with respect to the laity.

CHAPTER 4

Incarnation and Pentecost

You Should Know

- The first step toward a biblical doctrine of the Trinity is reading the Bible as a whole.

- The second of three interpretive moments required to comprehend the doctrine of the Trinity is consideration of the narrative unity of Scripture.

- The third of three interpretive moments required to comprehend the doctrine of the Trinity is recognizing the intentional self-revelation of God.

- Sabellianism: the heresy which confuses the divine persons by making the Son and the Spirit another form of the Father in action

- Modalism: the heresy that denies any personal distinctions within the divine being, so that "Son" and "Spirit" are one person who is also the Father. (p. 110)

- Arianism: the heresy that denies any personal distinction within the divine being, so that "Son" and "Spirit" must be creatures and not fully divine

- Generation or begetting: the eternal relation that obtains between the Son and the Father

- Spiration or breathing-out: the eternal relation that obtains between the Spirit and the Father

Essay Questions

Short

1. What main theological problem was Augustine trying to answer in his discussion of the Trinity? How did he go about addressing it? (p. 93–94)

2. Explain and summarize the two forms of heresy which deny that the historical missions of the Son and the Spirit reveal anything about the eternal being of God. How can they be nearly opposites and yet give the same answer to the question, "What do the missions of the Son and the Spirit reveal about God?"

3. What is the proper relation between the temporal missions of the Son and the Spirit and the eternal being of God?

Long

1. Looking back to the previous unit, summarize the three aspects of Scripture, and the corresponding three steps of comprehension, necessary to appreciate the biblical revelation of the Trinity.

Quiz

1. What was Aquinas's starting point in his exposition of the doctrine of the Trinity?
   a) The processions within the eternal Godhead
   b) The mission of the Son and the Spirit in history
   c) The experience of the different persons in salvation
   d) The ancient creedal traditions of the church

2. The task of understanding the Trinity from the historic missions of the Son and the Spirit requires all of the following understandings of Scripture *except*:
   a) Scripture as a whole is a witness to the Trinity.
   b) Scripture includes Christophanies throughout its revelation.
   c) Scripture is a narrative unity.
   d) Scripture constitutes God's progressive self-revelation.

3. What is the only claim that needs to be established to support the program of construing Scripture as a whole?

    a) Biblical writers were aware of writing canonical documents.

    b) Biblical writers were aware of their own divine inspiration.

    c) Scripture has a single divine author.

    d) Scripture presents itself as a literary unity.

4. What kind of perception is necessary to read the entire Bible as a larger unity?

    a) The ability to comprehend its texts as something actually unified and the ability to exhibit the marks of that unity

    b) The ability to discern both the different emphases within each Testament and the common theological themes across the Testaments

    c) The ability to tease out various redactional layers of biblical books and assign them to their respective historical contexts

    d) The ability to contemplate God in himself in prayerful reading and to experience God in himself in liturgical practice

5. Comprehending the narrative unity of Scripture involves being able to do what?

    a) Identify the diverse genres of Scripture and elucidate both their distinctiveness and their unity.

    b) Specify how Christ is active and present in the Old Testament narratives, and how his incarnational mission illuminates his activity in Israel's past.

    c) Grasp the central story line and comprehend God as its author and agent.

    d) Understand the role of the Spirit in the inspiration and production of Scripture.

6. What makes the third step in comprehending the doctrine of the Trinity the largest one?

    a) It moves from contingent facts of history to eternal and necessary truths.

    b) It moves from the experience of God as trinity in redemption
       to the reality of God as trinity in eternity.

    c) It moves from the plane of history to the transcendent plane
       of God's identity.

    d) It moves from the realm of systematic theology to the sphere
       of contemplation.

7. What is the fundamental task of Trinitarian theology?

    a) Explicating in a philosophically coherent way the internal
       relations of a three-in-one divinity

    b) Considering the central events of salvation history against
       the background of the eternal being of God

    c) Interpreting the events of the biblical story as the mighty
       acts of God

    d) Defending the doctrine that the Spirit proceeds from the Son
       as well as from the Father

8. What is a main weakness of the maximalist answer to the question
of what the missions reveal about God?

    a) There is no way to move from historical mission to the being
       of God.

    b) The identity of God is dependent on the world process.

    c) It denies the presence of God in the world.

    d) It carries out a form of negative theology.

9. What is the revelatory significance of the missions of the Son and
the Spirit?

    a) They make known the eternal processions of the Son and the
       Spirit.

    b) They show subordinationism and authority in the eternal
       being of God.

    c) They indicate that God is eternally suffering with and for his
       creation.

    d) They illustrate the different modes of being available to the
       one divine essence.

10. What is fundamental to Trinitarian exegesis?

   a) Recognition of Old Testament Christophanies
   b) Special attention to biblical Trinitarian formulas
   c) Use of the creeds as an aid to biblical interpretation
   d) The judgment that the two missions are manifestations of eternal relations

ANSWER KEY
1. A, 2. B, 3. D, 4. A, 5. C, 6. C, 7. B, 8. B, 9. A, 10. D

CHAPTER 5

God Who Sends God

You Should Know

- Relations of origin distinguishes the inter-Trinitarian persons from each other.

- The revealed names (Father, Son, Spirit) of God are the definitive, revealed, metaphorical summaries of the meaning of the divine missions.

- Two features that characterize the theological use of *person* as applied to the Trinity are metaphysical and ad hoc.

- The eternal processions of the Trinity can also, when translated into a new metaphorical register, be spoken of as actions.

- *Notae internae*: marks that distinguish the members of the Trinity and that belong to the divine essence

- *Notae externae*: marks that distinguish the members of the Trinity and that belong to the freely-chosen divine actions

- Generation and procession: the inward acts of the Trinity

- Incomprehensibility: the divine attribute that God cannot be grasped, defined, and made the object of full understanding

- Subordinationism: the heresy that results from making the generation of the Son and the procession of the Spirit something distinct from the being of God

- Incommunicability: the attribute of *personhood* that differentiates it from a *nature*

Essay Questions

Short

1. What is the relation between the revealed names of the different persons of the Trinity and the missions of the Son and Spirit?

2. Why is it impossible to argue to Trinitarian persons on the basis of divine attributes or actions?

3. What is the difference between the patristic way of speaking about God and the modern way of speaking about God, especially concerning the relation between God as he is in himself and as he relates to the world?

Long

1. What does the church mean when it calls God, "one being, three persons"? Why is it important that some things can be said of God substantially and some things can be said of God not substantially but relation-wise?

Quiz

1. Which of the following is the best way to describe each act of sending (of the Son and of the Spirit)?
    a) Each sending adds a new relation besides the processions.
    b) Each sending brings new complexity to the God-world relationship.
    c) Each sending confirms the accuracy of Old Testament prophecy.
    d) Each sending is the incorporation of a further ending point to an eternally existing procession.

2. What are the *notae internae* (marks or characteristics)?
    a) Characteristics of God belonging to the divine essence
    b) Internal memos, used metaphorically for inner-Trinitarian communication
    c) Marks that signify freely chosen divine actions
    d) Attributes of Christ's divine nature and his human nature

3. Without an account of divine action occurring within the being of God and among the Trinitarian persons, what is the most that theology can affirm about God's actions apart from his creation?

a) God is always creating.

b) God is doing nothing.

c) The relations within the Trinity are not best described as "actions."

d) God created the Son (Arianism).

4. What is one major result of not acknowledging the inward actions of the Trinity?

a) The aseity of God will assume a theological role that it cannot support.

b) The doctrine of the incarnation becomes an impossibility.

c) The role of human reason replaces trust in God's revelation.

d) The distinctions among the persons must be made on the basis of salvation history.

5. What must a theologian do if he or she wants to assert that the eternal relations among the persons are part of the being of God?

a) Explicate the Trinitarian creeds, especially that of Nicea (AD 325).

b) Provide Scriptural proofs that the Son and the Spirit are fully divine.

c) Demonstrate that the divine attributes are logically consistent with each other.

d) Give experiential evidence that God meets us as Father, Son, and Spirit.

6. Since God sent God and God, what common noun should be applied to each occurrence of "God"?

a) Person

b) Gods

c) Perichoresis

d) Being-in-becoming

7. Why cannot God be "Father" substantially?

   a) Because if he were, there would be no basis for the communication of attributes necessary for the real presence in the Eucharist
   b) Because if he were, there would be no basis for the Christophanies of the Old Testament
   c) Because if he were, the Son and the Spirit would also be the Father
   d) Because if he were, the Father would of necessity send only the Son and not the Spirit

8. What is the traditional theological language of the Trinity trying to express? (p. 140)

   a) The moral and psychological analogies between God and the human person that enable us to have true though limited understanding of God
   b) The soteriological connection between the economic and the immanent Trinity
   c) The transformation in our relationship to God brought about by the coming of Christ and the Spirit
   d) The extension of the missions of the Son and the Spirit into eternity past and future

9. What is the only way knowledge of God as subsisting in three persons is available to us?

   a) Through a method of biblical interpretation that is both critical and theological
   b) Through the salvation-historical extensions of those relations in the sendings of the Son and the Spirit
   c) Through the experience of God's saving presence, reflected on theologically and rationally
   d) Through an analysis of the meaning of *person* as known subjectively by humans

10. What is the most obvious advantage of the distinction between the immanent and the economic Trinity?

a) Its comprehensiveness
b) Its ability to move from the historical plane to the eternal one
c) Its didactic and heuristic use
d) Its mysterious quality

ANSWER KEY
1. D, 2. A, 3. B, 4. D, 5. B, 6. A, 7. C, 8. C, 9. B, 10. A

CHAPTER 6

Trinitarian Exegesis

You Should Know

- *Agraphon*: a teaching that is biblical though not explicitly stated in Scripture

- Matthew 28:19: the biblical passage that indubitably places three-ness in the biblical text

- A distinction made by Francis Turretin to explain the role of non-biblical language in theology: doctrine in Scripture according to sound and to meaning (or, *quoad sonum* and *quoad sensum*)

- The Johannine comma (or, the *comma johanneum*): the name for the traditional proof of the Trinity once thought to reside in 1 John 5:7

- The "Eastern mind": the ethnic stereotype that Hermann Reimarus blamed for the grandiloquent "manner of the Bible's expressions"

- Piecemeal proof: the method of demonstrating the biblical support for the Trinity by appealing to individual passages

- Relations of origin: the important aspect of Trinitarian theology that the piecemeal approach often de-emphasizes

- Attention to the economy of salvation as a whole: the crucial premodern interpretive practice necessary for demonstrating the doctrine of the Trinity

- Three elements present in the New Testament that provide the basis for biblical Trinitarianism: raw material, patterns, and pressure

- Worship and catechesis are two chief ends of Trinitarian theology in the Christian church.

Essay Questions

Short

1. Why is it insufficient to show that the doctrine of the Trinity is in harmony with the Scriptures?

2. Compare the use of the piecemeal approach by A. H. Strong and B. B. Warfield. What are their common tendencies and weaknesses?

3. What is the point of Prof. Sanders's extended parable of Albert Einstein? How does it relate to his argument concerning the effect of modern biblical scholarship on attempts to demonstrate the doctrine of the Trinity from the Bible?

Long

1. How clearly do you think the Trinity is revealed in the Bible? How would you answer the following challenge: "The doctrine of the Trinity is not clearly present in the Scripture. Therefore, it must be either rejected or accepted on the basis of some other authority, such as church tradition"?

Quiz

1. What is the fundamental task of dogmatics?
   a) The organization of biblical data into a coherent synthesis
   b) The discernment of the triunity of God in the biblical witness
   c) The defense of the faith through a robust apologetics
   d) The explication of Christian experience

2. To what biblical text does Gregory of Nazianzus appeal in order to demonstrate that the idea of threeness in God, whatever that threeness means, is biblical?
   a) The Priestly Blessing in Numbers 6:22–27
   b) The Baptism of Jesus in Matthew 3:13–17 and Luke 3:21–22
   c) The Lord's Prayer in Matthew 6:9–13
   d) The Baptismal Command in Matthew 28:19

3. To what does B. B. Warfield appeal in his justification of non-biblical language in Trinitarian theology?

    a) The traditional creeds of the church

    b) The rule of faith as a Trinitarian-shaped hermeneutical principle

    c) The need to preserve the truth of Scripture more than its words

    d) The simple faith of the common believer

4. The current crisis in Trinitarian theology has what as its root cause?

    a) The material change in the content of the doctrine

    b) The turn to subjectivity in modernity

    c) The decline in church attendance

    d) The epochal shifts in biblical interpretation that have reduced the available biblical arguments for it

5. What drove early modern Trinitarian exegetes, especially among Protestants, to scale back the range of biblical prooftexts (e.g., rejecting arguments based on messianic psalms)?

    a) The inroads of higher criticism

    b) The indisputable strength of Socinian arguments

    c) The complex interplay between nationalism, with its move toward unity on the political level, and the political commitments of theologians

    d) The intention to maintain the traditional doctrine on a more solid biblical basis

6. What strategy did Herman Reimarus employ to oppose the biblical basis of the main doctrines of Christianity?

    a) He gives basic biblical terms a meaning different from that given by orthodoxy.

    b) He attempts to show that the theological doctrines are philosophically incoherent.

    c) He denies the salvation-historical continuity between the Old and the New Testaments.

    d) He argues that Jesus was psychologically imbalanced.

7. Which of the following is a crucial element for renewing Trinitarian exegesis?

    a) A skillful use of modern historical methods
    b) Restoring the connections among the various parts of Scripture
    c) A fresh appreciation for the skill of patristic exegetes
    d) Rejecting the Enlightenment's epistemological conceits

8. In what way is the piecemeal approach to biblical Trinitarianism congenial to the character of the revelation of the Trinity itself?

    a) It places the emphasis on the theologian's attitude toward the subject matter.
    b) It attempts to read each biblical book as a discrete unity with its own internal coherence.
    c) It reflects the fact that the various propositions concerning the Trinity are scattered throughout Scripture.
    d) It respects the threefold structure of the pre-temporal, temporal, and eschatological revelation.

9. What is the main reason that B. B. Warfield provides only a weak treatment of the processions in his treatment of the Trinity?

    a) He wants to avoid Monarchianism.
    b) He wants to avoid subordinationism.
    c) His solution/crystallization illustration does not allow for it.
    d) His treatment is restricted in terms of space.

10. What premodern insight must be maintained for the validity of Trinitarian doctrine?

    a) The plausibility of allegorical exegesis
    b) The Athanasian slogan, "God became man, that man might become God"
    c) The ecclesiological rather than the academic context for doing theology
    d) The economy of salvation as a coherent whole

ANSWER KEY

1. B, 2. D, 3. C, 4. D, 5. D, 6. A, 7. B, 8. C, 9. B, 10. D

CHAPTER 7

New Covenant Attestation

You Should Know

- The resurrection is the event that gave to the incarnate Son that life which the Father eternally gives to the uncreated Son.

- The general effect of Augustine's and Luther's interpretation of Jesus's baptism is to reduce it to an educational event.

- The central text of Trinitarian theology is the dominical command in Matthew 28:19.

- Gregory of Nazianzus is the theologian who uses the threefold baptismal command ("the Father, and the Son, and the Holy Spirit") to indicate that the Christian theologian should seek Scripture to understand what these three refer to.

- Paul does not argue for a Christology or a Trinitarian doctrine; rather, assumes them.

- Johann Albrecht Bengel was an eighteenth-century exegete who mined Paul's epistles for the Trinitarian presuppositions behind them.

- John Davenant was a seventeenth-century exegete who read Paul's epistles in the context of a coherent biblical doctrine.

- Apostles' Creed: one of the earliest postbiblical attempts to make a theological statement on the basis of the New Testament

- Epiphany: traditional name for the manifestation of the Trinity at Jesus's baptism

- Social Trinitarianism: a modern theological tendency that emphasizes the multiplicity and difference within the Trinity

Essay Questions

Short

1. How does the salvation Jesus brings demonstrate the unity of his interactions with the Father and the Spirit? How is the eternal generation of the Son related to the resurrection of Jesus?

2. What is unique about the baptismal command in Matthew 28:19? What did Martin Luther mean when he calls the heavenly voice and the dove at Jesus's baptism "a reality and a symbol"?

3. How did John Davenant use Colossians 1:15 to make a distinction between divine persons and divine essence?

Long

1. What is the "Trinitarian life of Jesus"? How does the Gospel narrative depict the interrelations among the Father, Son, and Spirit?

Quiz

1. (T/F) Because the revelation of the Trinity most properly occurs in the actual sending of the Son and the Spirit, the New Testament should be considered a written attestation of that revelation.

2. Which best describes the character of the New Testament witness to the Trinity?
   a) Direct
   b) Oblique
   c) Progressive
   d) Nonexistent

3. Who are most obviously the main characters in the story of Jesus?
   a) Jesus, the Father, the Spirit
   b) Mary, Pilate, the Father

c) Jesus, Mary, Pilate

d) The Father, the Spirit, Peter

4. What does the baptism of Christ highlight?

   a) The dual procession of the Spirit from the Father and the Son

   b) The historical activity of the fellowship among the three persons

   c) The importance of believer's baptism by immersion

   d) The social equality of all three divine persons

5. According to Augustine, although the persons of the Trinity are distinct, their external works are _____.

   a) Also distinct

   b) Manifold

   c) Undivided

   d) Paradigmatic

6. (T/F) For Augustine, Jesus's baptism demonstrates the physical or local presence of the three persons of the Trinity, and thus proves their individual uniqueness.

7. (T/F) According to Luther, the signs given in the baptism of Jesus are the actual persons of the Trinity manifest in history.

8. Augustine and Luther represent a tradition in theology that recognizes Jesus's baptism as a verbal presence of the Trinity (e.g., not a manifestation of the actual Trinity). What instinct drives this tradition?

   a) The conviction that God is transcendent and beyond the categories of human language

   b) The sentiment that any substantive revelation in the baptism would confuse the distinction between the creator and the created

   c) The desire to avoid modalistic Monarchianism

   d) The need to maintain that the visible missions of the Son and Spirit reveal the Trinity

9. Gregory of Nazianzus shows that the Christian theologian is compelled to search the Scriptures looking for the Trinity on the basis of what?

    a) The rule of faith (anologia fidei)

    b) The Nicene and Chalcedonian Creeds

    c) The command of the risen Lord

    d) The experience of worship, which proceeds to the Father, through the Son, in the power of the Spirit

10. Which of the following statements best reflects Trinitarian theology as found in Paul?

    a) Trinitarian doctrine is the deep presupposition of salvation.

    b) Trinitarian doctrine is the rhetorical flair crowning Paul's discussion of salvation.

    c) Trinitarian doctrine is the explicit concern expressed in some of Paul's letters, but not others.

    d) Trinitarian doctrine can be found in the literary structure of Paul's epistles.

ANSWER KEY

1. T, 2. B, 3. A, 4. B, 5. C, 6. F, 7. F, 8. D, 9. C, 10. A

CHAPTER 8

Old Covenant Adumbration

You Should Know

- Adumbration: a word used to indicate the dimly lit character of the Trinity in the Old Testament

- Rereading: the practice of reading Scripture as a whole, allowing new layers of meaning to be discerned that move beyond the original meaning

- The Trinitarian hinge: the place where the prospective witness of the Old Testament to God and the retrospective witness of the New Testament converge

- Convergent hyperfulfillment: the way divergent trajectories witnessing to God's saving acts in the Old Testament are more-than-fulfilled in the missions of the Son and the Spirit

- Christophany: an Old Testament manifestation of divine presence (theophany) equated by Christian exegetes with the pre-incarnate Son

- Prosoponic exegesis: the practice of discerning the Trinity speaking through different speakers in the Old Testament

- Matthew Bates was a contemporary scholar whose work has brought the practice of prosoponic exegesis from patristics to biblical studies.

- Marie-Josèphe Rondeau was a contemporary scholar whose work has examined prosoponic exegesis of the Psalms in patristic writings.

- Hilary of Poitiers was a fourth-century Latin Church Father whose work *On the Trinity* made extensive use of prosoponic exegesis.

- *Gloria Patri*: Trinitarian praise used by Gerhohus the Great to conclude his interpretation of each of the psalms

Essay Questions

Short

1. What are the two possible approaches to outlining a Trinitarian theology that Prof. Sanders considers? What are the advantages and/or disadvantages of each? Which one does Prof. Sanders choose?

2. What role does Old Testament monotheism play in constructing the doctrine of the Trinity? How is it important for making ontological statements about God on the basis of the canonical narrative?

3. What understanding of revelation is the necessary prerequisite for the interpreter to move from exegesis to the doctrine of the Trinity? What were the early church's correct instincts with regard to this matter?

Long

1. What is prosoponic exegesis and how does it differ from reading Christophanies in the Old Testament? Do you think that prosoponic exegesis violates the clear grammatical-historical sense of the Old Testament? Is prosoponic exegesis valid if it affirms but goes beyond the grammatical-historical sense?

Quiz

1. According to Geerhardus Vos, the Old Testament does not offer a decisive proof for the doctrine of the Trinity. To support this claim he offers all of the following reasons *except*:

a) The Old Testament saints were not able to read in the Old Testament all that we are able to find there.
b) The Old Testament revelation was not completed but only preparatory.
c) During the Old Testament dispensation, the concept of God's oneness needed to be impressed.
d) The Old Testament revelation was properly concerned with matters of social organization and justice rather than speculative theology.

2. If the actual sending of the Son and the Spirit is the revelation of the Trinity, with the Old Testament acting as adumbration and the New Testament as witness, what corollary emerges concerning the use of the Old Testament as an anticipation of the Trinity?

a) The most productive study will examine where and how the prospective witness of the Old Testament and the retrospective witness of the New Testament overlap.
b) The best approach to the Old Testament will pay attention only to the forward-moving direction of the narrative, without reading later elements and events back into earlier ones.
c) The patristic exegetical strategies for reading the Old Testament are superior to modern historical-critical ones.
d) The ideal method of locating the Trinity in the Old Testament is to examine certain key theological words and their development.

3. The doctrine of the Trinity requires an understanding of revelation that holds what elements in their essential unity?

a) Experience (the liturgical paideia of the early church) and Spirit (the presence of God in community)
b) Act (all the events of the economy of salvation) and word (all the words of Scripture)
c) Love (the reality of God-for-us) and reflection (the illumination of the interpreter's mind)
d) Word (all the words of Scripture) and sacrament (all the legitimate practices of the church)

4. Which of the following statements best characterizes the locus of hyperfulfillment?
   a) It is properly a matter of christological fulfillment, although pneumatology does play a role.
   b) It is equally a matter of christological and pneumatological fulfillment.
   c) It is properly a matter of pneumatological fulfillment, although Christology does play a role.
   d) It is equally a matter of christological, pneumatological, and ecclesiological fulfillment.

5. Which of the following is true of Mark 1:2–3, providing substantive legitimacy to the practice of prosoponic exegesis?
   a) "God" speaks to the "Lord."
   b) The vision Isaiah had of God was actually a vision of the pre-incarnate Christ.
   c) The quotation in Mark actually comes from three Old Testament texts (Exodus 23:20; Malachi 3:1; Isaiah 40:3), suggesting three distinct divine sources.
   d) God's Spirit is poured out on the anointed one.

6. What makes prosoponic exegesis of the Old Testament a valid exegetical option for Christian interpreters?
   a) The advent of Christ and the Spirit
   b) The logos, which provides the metaphysical links for allegory
   c) The unity of God's external acts
   d) The typological correlation between signs and signified

7. What question can best guide prosoponic exegesis of the Old Testament, especially as it relates to Trinitarian reading of the manifestations of God's presence?
   a) "Which of these personifications is a distinct person?"
   b) "Does this manifestation clearly display the characteristics of the Son?"
   c) "Is there some kind of threeness present in the context of this manifestation?"
   d) "Can Christ and the Spirit be picked out retrospectively from among these manifestations?"

8. Properly done, what does prosoponic exegesis allow the interpreter to see in salvation history?

    a) The unity of justification and sanctification

    b) The correspondence between creation's blueprint in the mind of God and the eschatological kingdom of heaven

    c) The pattern of relations connecting the Father, the Son, and the Spirit

    d) The dialogue between the pre-incarnate Son, Satan, and the angels

9. What Old Testament passage is important for the way it brings together the New Testament interpretation of the Old, the enthronement of Christ, and prosoponic exegesis?

    a) Deuteronomy 32

    b) Psalm 110

    c) Isaiah 6

    d) Isaiah 53

10. Both modern scholars and patristic interpreters attempt to identify speakers in the biblical text. What important difference characterizes each approach?

    a) Modern scholars appeal to the category of mystery and progressive revelation, while patristic scholars interpreted the Old Testament as if it plainly revealed Christian doctrine.

    b) Modern scholars find the Old Testament material conducive toward a kind of incipient social Trinitarianism, while patristic interpreters avoided personalist categories.

    c) Modern scholars stay within the horizon of historical reconstruction, while patristic interpreters discerned relations among persons.

    d) Modern scholars have to deal with the problems of the Enlightenment, while patristic interpreters had to deal with the problems of polytheism.

CHAPTER 9

Theses on the Revelation of the Trinity

Essay Questions

1. How is the revelation of the Trinity related to the gospel and salvation?

2. What does the revelation of the Trinity say about God himself?

3. Why are words necessary for the revelation of the Trinity to occur?

4. How does the New Testament relate to the revelation of the Trinity?

5. In what sense is the revelation of the Trinity a revelation of something already occurring?

6. How does the revelation of the Trinity relate to the unity of the biblical canon?

7. What is the proper role of the discipline of systematic theology with respect to the Trinity?

Notes

www.ingramcontent.com/pod-product-compliance
Lightning Source LLC
Chambersburg PA
CBHW011747020426
42331CB00014B/3309